Three Moms from Hell

By James Nugent

Disclaimer of liability.

What follows is a frank discussion of abuse and the damage done by failed parents. It is not a pleasant or gentle discussion. It is not to be used as a substitute for mental health counseling.

The field of Psychology has failed in many areas but not in the area of abuse issues. A competent psychotherapist can be of great assistance in healing the damage done to by abuse and neglect. If you suffered abuse at any time in your life I strongly encourage you to seek competent help.

The life you save may be your own or that of your offspring. Then you will not end being a mom (or dad) from hell.

Important Note

I have taken great pains to sanitize all identifying characteristics from these very real people in the story. To use real names and such would only create more pain. This true book is about real people and real children. Any apparent connection between persons living or dead is purely unintentional and coincidental. It is the authors hope that by discussing these parental failures, and abuse victims will be motivated to get the professional help needed and move on to have high quality happy lives. Again, this is only a discussion and not a substitute for therapy.

Anne

So my old friend Anne lies on her death bed, in a semi-comatose state. She is suspended somewhere between the living and the dead. The doctors assure me that she can think clearly and hear everything said. She feels pain and especially boredom. She cannot voluntarily move even her eyes. She had a drunken car accident and a devastating head injury.

One of the of the last things she told me before she sank into the twilight of her life, was that she wished she could yank out the power cord to the respirator she has been attached to for 4 months. That machine was the only thing keeping her alive. However at the time she had lost the ability to use her hands or move her arms.

I told her now was the time to reflect and prepare to meet God. She ignored me and we continued to talk slowly about her life and her personal affairs. She was not surprised that her grown children had looted her home, stolen her jewelry, cash, appliances and were driving and selling her cars.

In a massive desperate attempt at denial she said, "Mommy has always been there for them so it's natural for them to take everything." It would be a good explanation except mommy has never been there for them. All through their childhood, all three children always came second or third or not at all, to mommy's sex life a drug/alcohol use.

She dragged them through five marriages and countless "boyfriends" and one night stands. Most all of her partners where emotionally, physically and or sexually abusive to the kids.

She says she took the abuse as much as they did. But she is not telling the truth. A child suffers more and becomes scathingly angry when all the pain they suffer comes from mom's irresponsibility. After a while they begin to just to try to look out for themselves, and truly hate their lives and the wretch they call mom.

Of course, that is one way the cycle of abuse and neglect is relentlessly passed on to the next generation. That thing you hate the most sets the stage for you to repeat the similar abuse in your life. Some 70% of abuse victims go on to abuse the next generation unless they get professional and sometimes lifelong therapy.

Anne suffered from her mom's irresponsibility. At thirteen, one of her mom's husbands impregnated Anne while mom watched. Anne was giving an abortion and sent away to live with another former husband of mom's. Anne was a self-medicating alcoholic and pot head by 14 years of age. The sex offender dad lived with mom for years.

Let us stop right here. Every generation has an excuse to pass on the abuse to the next generation. For example Anne's grandmother had a rough life as a teen prostitute in Seattle in the 1940's. In reality it is just an excuse.

Children should be protected and nurtured. The first and most important business of any marriage is for the complete and total wellbeing of the offspring. That is it. There is no explanation that will exonerate a parent from this sacred almost holy trust.

The only way the cycle of abuse will stop is when mommy puts aside her wants and needs for the good of the children.

The same goes for men but this is a true story of three moms from hell.

So let examine to damage done to her three kids.

The oldest child was her daughter Zoey. She is a physically beautiful young women in her late twenties. She has Post Traumatic Stress Disorder, Anorexia, and a drug problem. She highly sexualized, and so skinny she longer menstruates. She never graduated high school and has no job skill except in the sex industry.

The next son is moderately learning disabled and homeless. Mommy never stayed in place one place long enough for him to benefit from Special Education. He has had many problems in the street and sooner or later will turn up dead.

The third adult child is a workaholic and although he doesn't drink or do drugs he has a temper that gets him in trouble a lot with his wife and child and the police.

Will this cycle of abuse continue on? Yes, unless everybody dies and or the survivors get professional help. The abuse will be passed on like a diabolical curse to the next generation.

As Anne's respirator pumps night and day and she lies in a light coma; I can't help but think that at least she can't inflict anymore pain on anybody. Her children, mother and family never visit. They think their lives will magically get better when she is gone. Maybe she will finally find peace before she dies. I guess we will never know.

Kathy

Kathy was married in the 1950's and dutifully gave birth 10 times. Two babies were still born. She was a stay at home mom who most of the time did a reasonable job of taking care of her children's physical needs but failed to nurture the children emotionally. In fact she started to use the kids for her emotional amusement. It started by dressing the boys in girl's clothes and fixing their hair in bizarre Shirley Temple style.

She got such a kick out of that she played mind games with the young ones. She had degrading names for the boys and girls. Tommy became Tiffany. Tammy became odd Todd.

Sometimes when she was out "shopping" there would be little to eat in the house. The kids would resort to cracker and mustard sandwiches. Later when she would return she would serve grease laden gravy smothered fried chicken that would sicken hungry children. Other foods were often hideous. She thought it was funny. The kids ate what they were able to stomach.

Dad at the time was not present in the home very much. He worked hard as a Civil Engineer. When he would visit the home at night, even the pets would hide. Everybody knew that a screaming match would erupt. Dad usually left to go to the bar or beat his wife black and blue.

They were divorced and even managed to have their marriage annulled in the Catholic Church. Everybody agreed that it was a marriage that should have never happened.

Kathy broke her leg a year ago. She was acutely difficult and or abusive to the nursing home staff. She often made false claims of abuse especially about a nurse on the second floor who she alleged threaten her with a large knife in the night.

In reality there was no bearded nurse and no second floor in the facility. Kathy was just lonely and wanting attention. She was rarely visited by her children or even her grandchildren. They hated her.

So she decided to starve herself in order to try to get more visitors. She refused to eat for a time, but after a few weeks she would start again. This pattern went on for almost a year.

Along the way there were infections and organ failures, even surgeries. She continued to intermittently refuse to eat, and fewer visitors came.

I would visit Kathy once a week and we would talk about her life. Sometimes I could not look her straight in the eyes because she had a strange way of using her eyes in a "puppy dog" way. She had a way of drawing you into her lies. I never really understood her. One time she even flashed her breasts at me in order to get a reaction out of me. A nurse stopped her and I gave her a very disapproving scowl.

She was not offended or even irritated when her children stole her antiques for her modest home at the beach. Maybe she knew that she had no more control over her victims. Maybe in a way she was releasing them and was also free of her role as mom.

At one time Kathy had been a right wing fundamentalist Christian. But she neither understood are trusted religion now.

I was at her bedside a day before she died. I fed her ice chips and a spoon full of vanilla pudding. I asked her if I could read some scriptures to her. She loudly croaked, "no." I asked if I could pray silently at the foot of her bed. She didn't respond. So I read the Psalter while she stared at me with an angry face that look that looked like it could kill.

What was the damage done by a mom who used her children for sport and amusement? All but one became alcoholic. Several have mental illness. The have a family tradition of failed marriages.

Some the stories are bizarre. Like the sibling who married a cross dressing man. The man later admitted he was also homosexual. They got divorce. He still hangs out with one of the other siblings and brings his new wife, and his latest boyfriend.

One of the most alarming adult children is a psychopath called Tama. Kathy's daughter never married and named her one child a humiliating name that makes him a mockery wherever he goes. I suggested he legally change his name but he didn't want to offend his mom. His life has been hell and his mom has toyed with him all his life. She is in a word selfish to the extreme. Christmas presents would be returned for the money and Christmas trees were 6 inches tall. Every private and embarrassing moment in his childhood was fuel for her gossiping. Even her supposed friends reject her because she is too evil.

Her symptoms riddle almost all her siblings. She lies, steals and thrives off the pain of others. She gets a thrill by cleverly inflicting emotional pain.

Yes, Anna was a piece of work and I knew she would be dead in the morning. I cried when she died the next day but it was for all the pain she had cause in the lives of so many people.

Unless all her victims get help, her legacy pain of will live on and on.

Dew

Her name was Dew and I spoke for years on a monthly basis and twice the week before she died. She was college educated at a major Lutheran institution and received an undergraduate and Master's degree in psychology in only five years. She was an upstanding member of her local church and living off a generous state retirement. She was success in every way except one. She was dismal failure as a mom.

When the oldest child was twenty and the youngest was nineteen, her abusive alcoholic husband died of a stroke. Finally Dew was free. She had been was busy in a violent marriage and just never had time or energy for motherly nurturing.

Even though the children were nearly grown, they were emotionally starved for love and belonging. This would lead to decades of looking for love in all the wrong places. Basically they didn't know how to love or be loved. Neither did their mom.

It would take years of therapy and sometimes interventions from God to finally reduce their anxiety and depression.

Eventually the son would find a healthy relationship and pass that new and healthy legacy on to his children. The daughter did not do so well. She married and angry man who was somewhat emotionally delayed. She is presently looking to escape, but to what? She did not go to much therapy, so she does not have to tools necessary to avoid making the same mistakes with the choice of her next husband.

Whatever you are accustomed to, no matter how awful, is what makes you feel most comfortable. As a child you learned valuable tools, for survival. Being in a safe and happy relationship just may not feel right. You may not sure what to do!

A fear of wellness and kindness and love can be a terrifying experience. Wait, how can people fear love? In my 22 years as a counselor; clients often expressed discomfort when experiencing a healthy relationship for the first time. I always assured them that they would get acclimatized to it and ultimately enjoy it.

It is kind of like going swimming in a swimming pool. At first the warm water feels cold but after a few strokes you get used to it!

Most abuse victims have been swimming in ice water. That ice water that takes the joy out there life. It can prematurely take their lives.

I can't emphasize enough how important competent therapy is for abuse victims. Not just the victims you read about in the newspapers, but the victims of emotional neglect. The people whom never got love out of their mothers, suffer just as badly as the kid whom got beat.

Surprisingly in the last week of Dew's life there was an astonishing change. The woman who had been so acutely self-centered had changed. Before the change her son would be a basket case for days after talking to her. After the change he reported it was actually pleasant to talk to this mom from hell.

I have no idea what precipitated this change but it was extreme. One of the most profoundly selfish people I have ever met became thoughtful and caring in speech and action. I happened to speak to her again that week and she was definitely a changed woman.

Dew died five days after I spoke to her. I was asked by family members to be with them telephonically at her death bed. I noted for everyone's benefit how she had been so happy and loving the last time I talked to her. Then they pulled the plug on the respirator. I cried again for all the pain she had caused and all they pain she suffer through her 80 years.

Questions and Answers

Q. How did you happen to know three moms from hell?

A. I actually have known more, but since I turn 50 years old I have known a lot of sick and dying people.

Q. Isn't it disrespectful to call these women moms from hell?

A. It is a fairly accurate descriptor of their behavior.

Q. There no hope for failed moms?

A. There is always hope. Untreated there is not much.

Q. What can we do as a society?

A. Identify and stop abuse. Get treatment for all victims.

Q. It seems that child abuse and emotional abuse is growing?

A. Yes, it seems so and there is research that would indicate so. Locally in my county 1 in 3 girls and 1 in 4 boys is sexually assaulted before they are 18 years old.

Q. What about emotional neglect?

A. I know of no reliable research but most counseling practitioners agree that it is like a plague on society.

Q. Where will it all end?

A. Unless victims get treatment and then rise up to say "no," society will not function.

Q. Do you have a final comment?

A. If we don't do something different nothing will change.

Other Books by James Nugent

How I Sailed From Olympia to the San Juan Islands, and Returned Safely

An Alternative Boating Guide to Southern Puget Sound

How and Why I lived Aboard

Kayaking Budd Inlet in South Puget Sound

I Speak Esperanto

The Rainbow Road and Other Signs of God's Love

Living an Abundant Life, Within Your Means

Social Jujitsu and Powerful Principles for Managing Social Conflict

Blackjack on My Small Budget

A Little Benedictine Oblate Manuel

Without Speech

All things work

Loving Time with Your Creator

Personal Adventures in a Life of Learning

The Good News about Being Catholic

E-book Writing and Overcoming Barriers to Creativity

E-book Writing and Organizing Your Ideas

My Forty Days for Life 2013

Lifestyle Reality Observing

How to Sail in the Winter

How to Get Your Kid to Move Out

How to Get What Want

Sex, Abstinence, and Happiness

Cynthia Says Radio Show – Anger is a choice

Available at Amazon.com in Kindle E-Book and or Audible Book or Paperback

Reflections and Notes